CAROL M. HIGHSMITH AND TED LANDPHAIR

NEW YORK CITY
THE FIVE BOROUGHS
A PHOTOGRAPHIC TOUR

CRESCENT BOOKS

NEW YORK

PAGE 1: *The Statue of Liberty loomed for a short time over Paris itself while Bedloe's Island in New York Harbor was made ready. The frame supporting the statue was designed by Gustave Eiffel, later made famous by his Eiffel Tower in the French capital. The Manhattan skyline, viewed from Ellis Island (pages 2–3), looked nothing like this when most European immigrants arrived at the processing center in the years straddling the turn of the century. Although the city got its first modest high-rise in 1887, it was not until the 1930s that eye-popping skyscrapers like the Empire State and Chrysler buildings began to crowd into hundreds of blocks of Midtown. Completed in 1977, the twin 110-story towers of the World Trade Center now dominate the skyline.*

THE AUTHORS GRATEFULLY ACKNOWLEDGE
THE SERVICES, ACCOMMODATIONS, AND SUPPORT PROVIDED BY
HILTON HOTELS CORPORATION
AND THE
FORT LEE HILTON, FORT LEE, NEW JERSEY
IN CONNECTION WITH THE COMPLETION OF THIS BOOK.

———

This 1997 edition is published by Crescent Books, a division of Random House Value Publishing, Inc., 201 East 50th Street, New York, N.Y. 10022.

Crescent Books and colophon are trademarks of Random House Value Publishing, Inc.

Random House
New York • Toronto • London • Sydney • Auckland
http://www.randomhouse.com/

Printed and bound in China

Library of Congress Cataloging-in-Publication Data
Highsmith, Carol M., 1946–
New York City: the five boroughs / Carol M. Highsmith and Ted Landphair.
p. cm. — (A photographic tour)
ISBN 0-517-18330-7 (hc: alk. paper)
1. New York (N.Y.)—Pictorial works. 2. New York (N.Y.)—Tours.
I. Landphair, Ted, 1942– . II. Title. III. Series.
F128.37.H575 1997   96-43088
974.7´1043´0222—dc20   CIP

8   7   6   5   4   3   2   1

———

Designed by Robert L. Wiser, Archetype Press, Inc., Washington, D.C.

All photographs by Carol M. Highsmith unless otherwise credited: map by XNR Productions, page 5; Whitney Museum of American Art, page 6; Bettmann Archive, page 8; Hine Collection, New York Public Library, page 9; New York Historical Society, page 10; Avery Architectural and Fine Arts Library, Columbia University, page 11; Museum of the City of New York, pages 12–13; Brooklyn Historical Society, pages 14–15; Bronx County Historical Society, pages 16–17; Queens Historical Society, pages 18–19; Staten Island Institute of Arts & Sciences, pages 20–21.

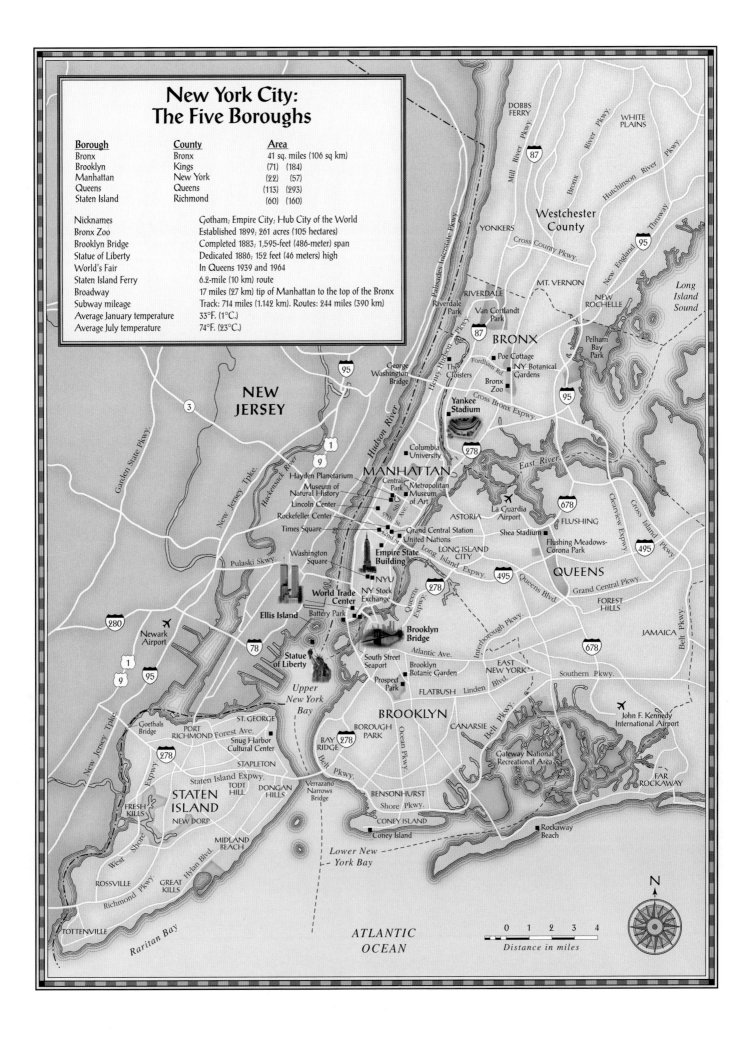

TO MANY PEOPLE, NEW YORK, THAT COLOSSUS OF ROADS, bridges, skyscrapers, and humanity, is America. From its pastoral beginnings, this city grew to encompass dozy villages and working farms, urban grandeur, and suburban sprawl. New York anticipated the America of today, becoming big, braggadocio, multicultural, materialistic. Long before it was positioned as a deliciously optimistic Apple, New York was known as the Big Onion, a grittier, more piquant, tear-inducing realm of many surprising layers. You can unpeel these overlays on the historical and architectural walking tours of the city that took the Big Onion name; they take you past Harlem churches that were once synagogues, the nation's largest Chinese Catholic church that was a Lutheran house of worship, whole neighborhoods that were German, Italian, East European Jewish, and then Chinese in turn.

Like the nation, New York has opened its arms to immigrants, then fretted that the new arrivals would ruin the culture. Peter Stuyvesant, the irascible, peg-legged governor of the Dutch West India Company's New Netherlands colony—which included most of what is now New York State, New Jersey, and parts of Delaware and Connecticut—complained constantly to his superiors in Holland about the riffraff he was asked to rule. The one thousand or so colonists in his capital, New Amsterdam on Manhattan Island, spoke eighteen different languages. Stuyvesant had Quakers tortured for their strange ways and English tongue, ousted Swedish interlopers from their Delaware River settlement, and led expeditions against neighboring Indians. But Stuyvesant could not hold back the English, who were busy gobbling up the northeastern corner of the New World. In 1664, without firing a shot, English Colonel Richard Nicolls convinced Stuyvesant to surrender New Netherlands without a fight. Nicolls immediately changed the colony's name to "New York" in honor of James, the Duke of York, who had dispatched his four warships. The English, however, would prove to be no more successful at suppressing the culture's polyglot influences, and the Americans who succeeded them rarely tried. Today more than 130 languages and dialects are heard in teeming New York.

Why did New York, and not Plymouth, Jamestown, or, for that matter, Philadelphia, Baltimore, or Boston, get to be the "world's capital city" and its acknowledged financial center, a towering axis of the arts, and the cramped home to nearly eight million people? In four words: pragmatism, rivers, moxie, and tolerance.

The Dutch already had a grip on the island that an unknown Englishman, who explored the Lower Hudson River two years before Henry Hudson arrived in 1609, had labeled "Manahatin." Dutch West Indias' agent, Peter Minuit, bought the entire island from Native Americans in 1626 for sixty guilders' worth of goods. That translates into a few hundred, or perhaps as many as one thousand, of today's dollars. Oliver E. Allen notes in *New York New York*, his comprehensive history of "The World's Most Exhilarating & Challenging City," that "to the Algonquin Indians who peopled the area, as to most Indians, land never belonged to any person or group, and all 'purchases' were regarded as temporary. The trouble was, the Indians never got a chance to renegotiate." Allen estimates the 1990 value of Manhattan real estate at $30 billion.

Most of the British colonies were founded as overtly religious enterprises, or as havens from Old World persecution. But from the beginning, New Netherlands was a business venture. Commerce, not ideology, has called the tune ever since. Poking around the coastline of North America on behalf of the Dutch in 1609, English explorer Henry Hudson marveled at the wide,

Joseph Stella's 1939 oil The Brooklyn Bridge: Variation on an Old Theme *is owned by the Whitney Museum of American Art. More than twenty workers died building the world's first steel suspension bridge— including its German-born designer, engineer John Roebling. Many laborers suffered attacks of the bends working in the underwater caissons that became footings for the bridge's towers.*

protected bays and harbors surrounding what would later be called Manhattan Island, and at the surprisingly deep water of both the river that soon would be named for him and the strait that would be misnamed the East "River." When Brooklyn and Staten Island and the other boroughs were brought within New York City's borders one day, 650 miles of generally ice-free oceanfront land were available for development and commerce. It later became clear that the Hudson River, combined with the ambitious Erie Canal being built upriver, would be the entrée to the natural resources of the Great Lakes and beyond. New York was ideally situated to dominate trade with Europe and the American heartland.

Moxie? In the 1890s, when Manhattan Island seemed full to capacity, before cities knew how to grow up as well as outward, its planners simply annexed their neighbors into five boroughs, instantly doubling the population and tripling the city's size. Not everyone submitted meekly. Brooklyn, a proud, independent city of 850,000 people, had been connected to Manhattan via the world's longest suspension bridge—*its* bridge, the *Brooklyn* Bridge—since 1883, and residents were divided over the referendum to create Greater New York. Brooklyn's business leaders favored the idea on the myopic assumption that they, with their bustling shipyards—and not Manhattan—would dominate the new megalopolis. Lightly settled Staten Island and the western villages of Queens, whose farmland was already Manhattan's vegetable garden just past Brooklyn out on Long Island, bought the idea because they foresaw improved roads and city services. (The even more rural eastern villages in Queens, however, declined the invitation and formed their own county, Nassau.) Most of the Bronx, to the north of Manhattan—the only piece of this grand, new New York actually on the U.S.

mainland—had already been annexed, so becoming a "borough" of the world's second-largest city (behind London) was taken in stride.

The men who schemed to create Greater New York, notably planner Andrew Haswell Green, the city's former comptroller, wanted New York to grow, for sure. But even more, they wanted the heavily Democratic city to control both sides of bridges that connected it with the rest of the mostly Republican state. And they wanted dominion over all the important harbors and wharves. Green had once ridden to the northern tip of Manhattan, gazed out upon the Bronx across the Harlem River, and daydreamed of bringing these "magnificent distances" under city control. Not incidentally, he pointed out later as he drew a circle roughly sixteen miles out from New York City Hall, expansion would reel in the riches of wealthy landowners who had established large country homes in New York counties just outside Manhattan to avoid paying city taxes. When the 320-square-mile city of 3.4 million people was finally realized in 1898, it instantly surpassed forty entire *states* in population. Ever after, Andrew Haswell Green would be called "The Father of Greater New York"

A Russian family await their turn to be questioned and examined by doctors at Ellis Island. By 1910 one million immigrants a year passed through the Registry Room en route to a new life.

by admirers and the devil incarnate by detractors, one of whom shot and killed him in 1903.

Peter Stuyvesant may have been cranky about the unseemly ethnic mix of his colony's population, but the color of money was the acceptable ticket of entry for entrepreneurs in several fields. Later, overseas shipping, trade with the interior, and the factories, banks, insurance operations, and investment companies needed to fuel them created an urgent demand for workers. Fortuitously, following the Irish potato famine of 1847 and the revolutions that rocked central Europe in 1848, hundreds of thousands of refugees showed up in New York. Finding jobs and neighborhoods of people like themselves, many stayed. By the time the Statue of Liberty rose in New York Harbor in 1886, many of the "huddled masses, yearning to breathe free" were already living in Manhattan tenements. From then until World War I, almost three-fourths of the twenty million immigrants who arrived in the United States landed in New York. Millions never left. Originally, aliens were processed at the Battery, the fort at the southern tip of Manhattan. But in 1892, two years after the federal government took over the processing of immigrants, the operation was moved to Ellis Island, not far from the Statue of Liberty in the Upper Bay. As these newcomers scrambled to get a foothold in the city, there would be profound tensions, even armed battles, based as often on religion as ethnicity. But most New Yorkers then, as now, got along because they had to if they were to make their way in this congested, competitive place.

To Brooklyn's dismay, Manhattan remained the core of the Big Onion. In 1883, when the Brooklyn Bridge opened across the East River, its 271-foot-high western tower was the tallest structure on Manhattan Island. Four years later on Broadway, architect Bradford Gilbert erected the thirteen-story Tower Building on a plot barely twenty-one feet wide. If Gilbert could do it, so could others, and by the turn of the century the skyline of Manhattan was changed from a low-slung conglomeration of ships' masts, church steeples, row-house roofs, and squat factories into a panorama of towers reaching high into the sky.

To be sure, these were modest skyscrapers compared with what was to come in the 1930s, when the 77-story Chrysler Building became the world's tallest structure for a year, until the

The Dakota, the first grand apartment on Manhattan's Upper West Side, had the countryside to itself when it opened in 1880. It was truly "out west" in wide-open spaces, beyond Central Park skaters.

104-story Empire State Building was completed. By then, even the city's fanciest apartment buildings were high-rises. Subways, which began operation on a single line in Manhattan in 1904, soon extended along twenty-eight stations to 145th Street in the northern neck of the island. Subway service opened to the Bronx in 1905, to Brooklyn in 1908, and in Queens in 1915. No one even considered stretching rail transit to remote Staten Island, which was well served by ferry and wished for no other urban tentacles. More than anything else, the subway facilitated the mass relocation of population in New York. Before long, even in far-out Bronx and Queens, village lines were blurring as new developments filled the empty spaces between them.

The frantic pace changed the culture as New York grew into the hub of world capitalism. The sounds of clattering trains, pounding jackhammers, snarling bulldozers, screaming sirens, and honking cars and taxicabs became background noise. Waves of ethnic succession rippled up Manhattan and then into the outer boroughs. In Hell's Kitchen, long an Irish settlement on the West Side, Hispanics predominate today. Where five hundred thousand Jewish garment workers, bakers, and pickle-shop owners and their families once crammed into the Lower East Side, fewer than fifty thousand Jews remain, the others replaced by Chinese and West Indians. Little Italy— which three generations ago was Little Ireland—has been nearly subsumed by Chinatown.

The maniacal pace of life in Manhattan is no stereotype. As Polish-born Yiddish folklorist Isaac Bashevis Singer said of New York in 1986, "This metropolis has all the symptoms of a mind gone berserk." There's a cab to catch, an important meeting, a subway due any second. It's a tough town, buddy. Most New Yorkers are not rude. In fact, if you can get their attention, they're among the most helpful, tenderhearted souls in the land. They're preoccupied, lost in their thoughts, trying to make a go of things.

"So now we come to New York City," wrote John Gunther in *Inside U.S.A.* in 1947, when the city was serene by comparison. It is, he said, "the inferno with no out-of-bounds, the supreme expression of both the miseries and the splendors of contemporary civilization." It is those splendors, say New Yorkers, that make the irritants of life in a megalopolis worth tolerating.

And worth visiting, starting with Liberty Island, 1.5 miles south of Manhattan Island. There, the torch of the hammered-copper statue that was first called *Liberty Enlightening the World* reaches 151 feet into the air. Frédéric Bartholdi's 225-ton Statue of Liberty was a gift from the people of France to mark the United States centennial of 1876. In her left hand, Lady Liberty clutches a stone tablet, on which is written, "July 4, 1776." It would be a decade after the centennial year, however, before the statue would be ready for President Grover Cleveland's dedication. Today, hardy tourists often eschew the twenty-two-story elevator ride and trudge up the 354 steps to the statue's crown. A ferry stop away at Ellis Island, closer to the New Jersey shore, visitors can imagine the emotions of the seventeen million immigrants who sat with their families and bundles of possessions in the great hall of the federal immigration facility between 1892 and 1954. The 1996 *Fodor's* guide to New York pointed out that 40 percent of all Americans in the 1990s were descendants of those men, women, and children who passed through Ellis Island's "golden door."

Manhattan has often been defined by its procession of skyscrapers, notably the Empire State and Chrysler buildings and the twin World Trade Center towers. But a symbol better loved by New Yorkers themselves is the 843-acre Central Park, the city's playland. Landscape architects Frederick Law Olmsted and Calvert Vaux transformed a wretched swamp into a masterfully cultivated oasis of lawns, gardens, ponds, trails, castles, and even a small zoo. Picnicking, miniature golf, birdwatching, a ride on a carousel (moved from Coney Island), chess, ice-skating, croquet, and lawn bowling are just a few of the park's pleasurable distractions.

New York's reputation as the cultural heart of the nation takes root right alongside Central Park, with the Metropolitan Museum of Art. This treasurehouse of priceless art—arguably the city's top tourist attraction—also encompasses the stunning exhibit of Middle Ages art, artifacts, and architecture that are housed in the Cloisters, the Met's indescribably amazing 1938 medieval-style annex high on a hill in Fort Tryon Park in far north Manhattan.

The main Metropolitan Museum building is the centerpiece of "Museum Mile," a breathtaking array of legendary cultural institutions between, roughly, East 70th and East 104th streets on and near Fifth Avenue. Among them are the Frick Collection, the Guggenheim Museum, the Museum of the City of New York, the Jewish Museum, and the Whitney Museum of American Art. Many of the great institutions are housed in the "Millionaires' Row" mansions once owned by turn-of-the-century industrialists. Across the park, the parade of cultural landmarks includes the American Museum of Natural History, the Hayden Planetarium, the Museum of American Folk Art, and the city's principal performing-arts palace, Lincoln Center.

A thorough architectural tour of Manhattan could take weeks.

Lewis Hine captured this photograph of men perilously (and bravely) at work assembling a skyscraper's steel skeleton, high above Manhattan's rooftops. It was a sight that would become commonplace in the early 1930s throughout the world's burgeoning commercial capital.

By 1936, when Berenice Abbott captured The Night View, *New York had become the world's greatest city of lights. Thomas Edison had generated electricity from a plant on Pearl Street as early as 1882, and by the 1930s most of Manhattan's wires had been buried underground.*

Where to start? The 1911 Beaux Arts masterpiece New York Public Library? The ornamented and lovingly restored Grand Central Terminal? Daniel Burnham's wedge-shaped, terra-cotta-clad Flatiron Building? Gothic Saint Patrick's Cathedral or any of a score of other magnificent churches, mosques, or synagogues? The theater is a Manhattan tourist magnet, of course, though few of the buildings on, off, and off-off Broadway are much to look at from the outside. Options for the restaurant portion of a "night on the town" are so numerous that guestimators stopped counting the number of Manhattan eating establishments at fifteen *thousand.*

Neighborhoods themselves have become tourist attractions, starting in Lower Manhattan. The 1950 U.S. Census found fewer than five hundred people living amidst the area's capitalist canyons. It was a ghost town of urban tumbleweeds as pages of the *Times* and *The Wall Street Journal* wafted down deserted streets. By the mid-1990s, thanks to extensive landfilling and the conversion of old office buildings to luxury condominiums, the population had soared past twenty thousand. SoHo (the district south of Houston Street) and TriBeCa (the triangle below Canal Street) were once grungy industrial tenement districts. Now they are hot spots equal to Greenwich Village, full of galleries, trendy restaurants, and loft buildings. On the streets of the Upper East Side neighborhood where brownstones and other gloriously detailed mansions have been converted to luxury apartments, conversations often turn on the amount of rent their tenants must be paying. Farther uptown, Harlem, built as a luxury suburb for which a market among the upwardly mobile never developed, is today home to six hundred African-American and Hispanic churches. Harlem is a study in contrasts—the lively streetlife near the Apollo Theater on West 125th Street, the quiet dignity of the brownstone row houses near the Abyssinian Baptist Church, and adjacent blocks of poverty-stricken neighborhoods.

There's a "different world" across the Brooklyn or Manhattan bridge in Brooklyn, observed writer Kennedy Fraser in a *New Yorker* magazine essay in July 1996. "Roses smell sweeter in Brooklyn [and] even the birds sound innocent, like youths from the old neighborhood singing a cappella." Brooklyn is the city's most nostalgic borough, reminiscing to this day about "dem Bums." They were the Dodgers—named for the nimble "trolley dodgers" who wove their way past Flatbush streetcars—the borough's very own major-league baseball team, playing at Ebbets Field. They may have been "bums," but they were *Brooklyn's* much-loved bums. When the Dodgers, along with the Giants of uptown Manhattan, left for lucrative California in 1958, only the Yankees in the Bronx were left, later to be joined by the Mets in Queens. Without its team and major-league cachet, Brooklyn fell into a period of civic mourning from which some say it has never recovered.

Like the other outlying boroughs, *Breuckelen* was founded as a place for the Dutch to build country manor homes and truck farms. Ferry service was spotty, even after the English took control, until Robert Fulton demonstrated his new steamboat in 1807. Brooklyn was but one of six independent towns on the western tip of Long Island that the English named "King's County." Five had originally been Dutch; the sixth, Gravesend, on the southern shore where Coney Island would later appear, was settled by English colonists led by a woman, Lady Deborah Moody. Brooklyn's city center grew in the heights across from Manhattan, and enclaves of stately brownstones in neighborhoods arose in Cobble Hill and Park Slope. Brooklyn was inundated by immigrants, first by Irish and Germans in the 1830s. It was poor Irish—already speaking English with a brogue and trying to cope with American idioms and the remnants of Dutch—who first developed the "Brooklyn accent." Comedians and Hollywood characters like the "Bowery Boys" greatly exaggerated it: "Youse meet me at Toity-toid and Toid Av'nue."

So fiercely did Brooklyn trumpet its self-sufficiency, even after it had lost its independence, that other New Yorkers talked about the bristling "Brooklyn attitude," and billboards could be found into the early 1990s welcoming visitors to "America's Fourth-Largest City." For decades, its docks and marine terminals were more than a match for Manhattan's; the famous Union ironclad warship *Monitor* was built in Brooklyn and launched at Greenspoint in 1862. Brooklyn earned New York City's first official landmark designation for the Pieter Claesen Wyckoff House, a 1766 Dutch colonial farmhouse where Hessian soldiers were quartered during the American Revolution. Brooklyn Heights was Greater New York's first recognized historic district. And if not a landmark, Floyd Bennett Field, the modest airfield that juts out into Jamaica Bay, should be on any trivia-lover's tour. It was there in 1938 that Douglas "Wrong Way" Corrigan took off on a flight for California and ended up, twenty-eight hours later, in Ireland.

Brooklyn also has its own spectacular 526-acre greensward, Prospect Park, designed by Olmsted and Vaux, the same men who created Central Park. Long revered as the "City of Churches," Brooklyn offers a full day's tour of impressive houses of worship. To mention just one: the Plymouth Church of the Pilgrims, which opened in the Brooklyn Heights in 1850, was

"Automats" were perfect for busy, often preoccupied, New Yorkers. Selection was immediate, and there was minimal human interaction needed. Delis and fast-food restaurants, serving fresher meals, helped put automats out of business.

the home church of fiery abolitionist Henry Ward Beecher. Many of Brooklyn's cultural attractions are world-caliber. The Brooklyn Academy of Music is the oldest continuously active performing-arts center in the nation. The Brooklyn Botanic Garden, across Flatbush Avenue from Prospect Park, is noted for its Cherry Esplanade, Garden of Fragrance for the visually impaired, and a section devoted to plants mentioned in the works of Shakespeare. The Brooklyn Museum has a renowned collection of Egyptian, pre-Columbian, and American art. And the Brooklyn Historical Society has one of America's most comprehensive local-history collections. At the New York Transit Museum—built in an abandoned subway station in downtown Brooklyn—visitors can linger in vintage subway cars, study the subways' engineering and control network, and try out a variety of early turnstiles and fare devices. The highest point in the borough is a hill in Green-Wood Cemetery, "Brooklyn's Garden City of the Dead," which is almost as large as Prospect Park. Its incredible, Gothic iron gateway was designed in 1861 by Richard Upjohn. Among those buried at Green-Wood are cowboy actor W. S. Hart; Tammany Hall ringleader Marcy "Boss" Tweed; and Frank Morgan, who played the title role in Hollywood's *The Wizard of Oz*.

Brooklynites will tell you their street festivals are less contrived and commercial than those in Manhattan, and that the delicatessens along Flatbush Avenue are as delightfully idiosyncratic as ever. Abandoned and burned-out high-rises of Bedford-Stuyvesant have been replaced by viable one- and two-family houses. Even Coney Island, bordered by housing projects and once thought incorrigibly tacky, is bright, bouncy, and fun again. Next door, New York's Aquarium for Wildlife Conservation celebrated its one-hundredth anniversary in 1996 with the opening of Sea Cliffs, a three-hundred-foot-long re-creation of the rocky Pacific Coast. And what bet-

ter signs could there be for Brooklyn, say supporters, than the development of a lively arts scene in Red Hook, once thought to be a dangerous and even sinister place? Or the movement of the Brooklyn Beer Company's operations into the borough? For years, brewing of the popular microbeer had been contracted out to an outfit in Utica, New York. Maybe the best sign of all for Brooklyn, in the face of reports of middle-class flight to Staten Island and elsewhere, is the ever-increasing rush-hour congestion in both directions on the Brooklyn Bridge: not just a backup of automobiles, but of pedestrians, bikers, and in-line skaters of every economic station, coming to Brooklyn to work, or heading home to Brooklyn after a day of toil in Manhattan.

The Bronx got its unusual name from the area's first settler, Danish immigrant Jonas Bronck. The Bronck family had clout, and everyone down in New Netherlands referred to "The Broncks' farm." While Bronck and his neighboring Dutchmen were busy settling the western side of the peninsula along the Hudson and Harlem rivers, the English were moving down from Connecticut and into the eastern section along Long Island Sound. One new arrival was Anne Hutchinson, daughter of a Puritan minister, whose descriptions of divine revelations so offended the starchy elders of the Massachusetts Bay Colony that they expelled her. She met a similar fate in Rhode Island and on Long Island before settling in Pelham Park in the Bronx. There, in 1643, Indians massacred her and most of her household. It is for her that the Bronx's Hutchinson River Parkway is named. With the building of King's Bridge over the Harlem River around 1700, the Bronx became New York's mainland connection. Farm-fresh produce soon found its way onto Manhattan Island, as did fresh water, piped in from clear springs. Until the twentieth century, the Bronx remained a land of farms, manor homes, and modest factories, including a snuff mill whose remains can still be found at the New York Botanical Garden.

Much of the Bronx had already been annexed by the time of the Greater New York initiative in 1898. Although many of the towns that were left, east of the Bronx River, voted against the idea, the section was annexed anyway.

The Bronx was one of the first parts of New York to succumb to rampant subdivision and apartment construction that would eventually lead to an oversaturation of low-income housing and to the abandonment and devastation that would scar the borough. The cycle began as wealthy landowners sold off their Bronx manors in favor of places in the "real" country, farther out in Westchester County. Middle- and working-class families filled the manor sites, newly subdivided, and, later, the high-rise cities that rose in the Bronx. When these people prospered enough to move to the Westchester or New Jersey suburbs, there was no solid base to replace them. So low did demand for Bronx units fall in the 1970s that many owners simply abandoned their properties, leaving them to the predations of vandals and drug dealers.

With the abandoned buildings, rising crime, and falling population came a withdrawal of services by a city that was, at the time, teetering on bankruptcy. The Bronx's big courthouse was moved to safer ground, as was the original borough hall. New York University moved out of its Bronx campus, leaving behind its stunning Hall of Fame ring of busts of prominent Americans; these sculptures are now a featured attraction at the Bronx Community College, which took over that NYU campus. About the borough's only ray of sunshine through the long and buffeting storm was the unifying force of the hometown Yankees. But even they were no longer the proud "Bronx Bombers," and they and their fans endured some woeful seasons before baseball's most storied team would challenge for a pennant again.

Compared with the bleak days, "the Bronx is up" today, not just geographically and in the song, but also in spirit and in hundreds of other tangible ways. Much of the blight is gone, replaced by promising developments of one- and two-family units. City and private colleges and topflight medical centers—including Fordham University and the Albert Einstein College of Medicine—have formed a steady employment base and brought bright minds into the borough. The Grand Concourse, a string of 1930s Art Deco residential buildings along a four-and-a-half-mile spine of the Bronx, has been largely renovated and cleaned. City Island, the Bronx's New England–style community of marinas and seafood restaurants, has added art galleries, museums, and delightful antique stores. The first four houses of the Historic House Trust tour of New York, including the home where Edgar Allan Poe wrote some of his greatest works, are in the Bronx.

Two of New York's finest cultural fixtures, the Bronx Zoo and the New York Botanical Garden, are thriving. The zoo, run by the Wildlife Conservation Society, marked a century of saving wildlife in 1995. At 265 acres the largest urban wildlife park in the nation, the Bronx Zoo redefined its role into a long-term repository for vanishing species and perpetuating rare and endangered creatures via exhibits like "Wild Asia," a baboon reserve, and a "Himalayan Highlands Habitat." And it added a summer-season "Butterfly Zone," with nearly one thousand butterflies flying freely in colorful flower gardens. Not far away, the New York Botanical Garden literally rebuilt itself as part of an $89-million, seven-year capital-construction program, updating its giant conservatory and adding horticultural exhibits and several programs

Early in the twentieth century, the men of the Clason Point Volunteer Life Saving Service in the Bronx saved drowning swimmers and went after foundering boats on Long Island Sound and the East River.

Director D. W. Griffith shot interior scenes for some of his movies on the set of the Biograph Studios, one of the nation's largest pre-Hollywood studios, on 175th Street in the Bronx.

of environmental education. The botanical garden even created a "children's corner," featuring "science-to-go" projects, a maze made from flowers, and "garden games" in which children solve plant and garden mysteries. In more ways than one, the Bronx never looked so good.

Admirers of Queens, the largest and most residential borough of all with more than 165,000 single-family homes, talk of the neighborhood identity that has lingered through decades of rapid urbanization. Flushing, Floral Park, Long Island City, and dozens of other individual Queens communities retain their individuality—including their own post office designations. Three of the most fascinating are Steinway, Jackson Heights, and Long Island City. Steinway was a company town built by German immigrant Wilhelm Steinweg, who Americanized his name after his brilliance at building pianos was affirmed. Some of Steinway's row houses are still in use, and the company still crafts pianos at a factory in another part of Queens. Jackson Heights was America's first large-scale co-op garden apartment community. On rolling farm-land, developer Edward MacDougall and architects A. J. Thomas and George Wells created blocks of massive apartment complexes that they opened to carefully screened upscale buyers. Each included spacious, beautifully landscaped courtyard common gardens. Today, several buildings in Jackson Heights are as elegant—and their gardens as manicured—as they were when they opened in the 1920s. Once grimy and industrial, Long Island City along the East River has become a surprising arts center. Its ten-stop "Art Loop" includes the Socrates Sculpture Park, an exhibition of large-scale outdoor art with the Manhattan skyline as a backdrop; the American Museum of the Moving Image, which explores the impact of film, television, and video on culture and society; and the International Design Center New York, a complex of more than one hundred showrooms displaying interior furnishings and architectural products.

Many Queens neighborhoods are twentieth-century creations, their modest homes built to satisfy the demand of returning veterans of World Wars I and II. Even after the last farmers departed for Nassau or Suffolk, farther out on Long Island, the New York City Department of Parks and Recreation retained a forty-seven-acre vegetable farm and orchard in eastern Queens as a working farm museum with a barnyard and fields open to visitors, including amazed inner-city schoolchildren, year-round. The farmhouse of the Queens County Farm Museum dates to 1772, a full 111 years before the county was established.

Queens's population explosion was stoked by two world's fairs held in Corona Park in Flushing Meadows in 1939–40 and 1964–65. The first was organized around the Trylon, a conical column 727 feet tall, and the Perisphere, a giant globe, which—along with demonstrations of wonders like television—symbolized "The World of Tomorrow." The centerpiece of the '64 fair was another globe, the "Unisphere," a 140-foot-high structure representing "Peace Through Understanding." The Unisphere still stands, a stone's throw from Shea Stadium and the National Tennis Center. So does a wave-shaped pavilion that is today the New York Hall of Science, the city's only hands-on science and technology museum. An equally fascinating remnant of the 1964–65 fair is the incredible Panorama of the City of New York, the world's largest architectural model, which today fills a spacious room at the Queens Museum of Art in Corona Park. Built by Lester Associates, Inc., for the New York City Pavilion, it depicts 895,000 individual miniature structures at the scale of one inch to one hundred feet. Not just familiar bridges and skyscrapers are identifiable and periodically updated. So are smaller office and

As New York's most residential borough, Queens has been a collection of definable neighborhoods that are still recognized by the U.S. Postal Service. Businesses like this hardware store served surrounding two- and three-story homes— and later mile after square mile of apartment buildings.

apartment buildings, and even houses, in their exact locations in all five boroughs. In 1996, the Queens Museum added a spectacular collection of Tiffany lamps, globes, and windows, acquired from the Egon and Hildegard Neustadt Museum of Tiffany Art. This was a coup, since Louis Comfort Tiffany designed and manufactured the Tiffany lamps in the nearby Corona neighborhood.

The most energetic mover behind the '64 world's fair was the indefatigable planner Robert Moses, "czar" of the city's vast park system who also wore more than ten other official city and state hats during his career. Moses's authority extended to bridges and highways, and he used the fair as a *raison d'être* for building expressways across Queens that produced an enormous boom in residential development. Traffic often backs up on the roads to Kennedy International Airport and LaGuardia Airport, which together cover almost five thousand acres of Queens and contribute more than $25 billion in economic activity. It's little wonder that aviation is the borough's largest industry.

Nowhere in New York City has the impact of a new tunnel, bridge, or expressway been as dramatic as it has in Staten Island. Through most of its history, hilly Staten Island, fourteen miles long and eight miles wide, had been almost an afterthought. It was thirty-seven years after the Dutch settled New Netherlands—after repeated bloody battles with recalcitrant Indians—before they got a foothold on *Staaten Eylandt* [State Island]. The English who soon supplanted them called the place "Richmond" after a duke of that time. Richmond was both its borough and county name until the borough title was changed to Staten Island in 1976. The story goes that Borough President Bob Connor got tired of hearing the other borough presidents ask him, "How are things down South?"—as in Richmond. Well into the twentieth

A turn-of-the-century parade in Queens underscores the maxim that all politics is local. Although Tammany Hall's influence was beginning to wane, aldermen still controlled lucrative patronage jobs—there was no civil service system—including police positions.

Grymes Hill, Stapleton. STATEN ISLAND, N. Y.

Grymes is one of several hills on once-bucolic Staten Island. First connected by bridge to New Jersey, the island endured an explosion of development when the Verrazano-Narrows Bridge to Brooklyn opened in 1964.

century, residents were islanders in temperament as well as fact, savoring their serenity at night and on weekends after ferry rides to work in Manhattan. They were tied to New York City financially, but to New Jersey by the 1928 Goethals Bridge. There was plenty of open space around Staten Island's sixty-two separate villages full of single-family homes and seashore cottages. Life on Staten Island was pleasant, safe, undisturbed by the intrusions of urban life.

Then in 1964, the city completed the Verrazano-Narrows Bridge, named for the Italian Giovanni da Verrazzano, who, exploring for Francis I of France, first sailed into New York Bay in 1524. The bridge spanned the channel between Brooklyn and Staten Island, changing Staten Island forever. In the classic pattern of moving out and up, tens of thousands of Brooklynites (and others) moved in, seeking a piece of Staten Island's tranquillity. In the next twenty years, the population would almost double, reaching four hundred thousand. An expressway connecting the Verrazano and Goethals bridges cut the island in half, and developers moved fast into the whole island, throwing up apartment and condominium complexes. Staten Island was soon dotted with strip shopping malls and freestanding fast-food restaurants as well. Off the expressway, the city's winding roads like Victory Boulevard and Amboy Road simply could not handle the surge in traffic.

But it was another indignity that inflamed Staten Islanders. In 1948, the city had begun to dump garbage into a landfill in the island's Fresh Kills wetlands. The promise, and everyone's expectation, was that the dumping would be short-term and small in size. But almost fifty years later, the scows were still docking, and the trucks rumbling, depositing fourteen thousand tons of refuse a day at Fresh Kills. When the landfill reached two thousand acres, it could be seen from space.

With all the assaults on the traditional way of life in Staten Island, some longtime residents left for New Jersey and beyond. But most stayed, still enamored of the island's many old, and some new, charms: despite some overbuilding, its 75 percent preponderance of single-family homes; a lively arts and humanities council that presents free concerts and other performances, several times a month, all over the island; Historic Richmond Town, a one-hundred-acre com-

Happy Land Park, South Beach, S. I.

Brooklyn's Coney Island was New York City's most famous amusement park, but remote Staten Island had its own playland, Happy Land Park, before the island was connected to the rest of the city.

plex of authentic seventeenth- through nineteenth-century schools, farmhouses, and shops— including a meticulously restored general store; a variety of venerable homes, including the Conference House, where three delegates to the Continental Congress, including Benjamin Franklin, unsuccessfully tried to talk British Admiral Lord Howe into a cease-fire; its own zoo and botanical garden; Snug Harbor, an 83-acre complex of museums, gardens, artists, performance spaces, and the island's own children's museum on the site of Sailors Snug Harbor, founded in 1831 as a haven for "aged, decrepit and worn-out sailors"; and, thanks to its hilly terrain, some of the best views of Staten Island's own waterfronts and bridges, and the Brooklyn and Manhattan skylines.

In every New York City borough, change has brought stresses and challenges. Indian, Vietnamese, Hispanic, African-American, and Russian neighborhoods have sprung up where Greeks, Italians, European and Syrian Jews, and Anglo-Saxons had once carved out enclaves. Demographers in New York in the mid-1990s were predicting a city at the turn of the century that would be 30 percent black non-Hispanic, 30 percent Hispanic, 10 percent Asian, and just 30 percent white. "We're a social laboratory," one Bronx resident told *American Way* magazine. Old-time New Yorkers worry still about immigrants taking away jobs, eating away at the tax base, abusing welfare, introducing strange foods fused from multiple cultures, and turning the sidewalks into a babel of confusion. But for all the complaining, the brashness, cynicism, and gruffness, New York eventually accepts them all. As American librettist Moss Hart put it in the 1959 play *Act One,* "The only credential the city asked was the boldness to dream. For those who did, it unlocked its gates and its treasures, not caring who they were or where they came from." Hunter College history professor Ed O'Donnell, who co-founded the Big Onion Walking Tours, points out that today's Vietnamese, Haitian, Iranian, or Indian immigrants to New York are self-selected. They could have gone elsewhere, but like the Irish or the Italians, the Czechs or Germans or Russian Jews of a century ago, they chose to come to New York, to bring new energy to the challenge of the most heterogeneous, hard-driving, self-absorbed city in America. Surely, if they can make it here, they can make it anywhere.

OVERLEAF: Immigrants sailed past the inspiring Statue of Liberty, whose full name is Liberty Enlightening the World. *The 151-foot-high statue became a symbol of freedom not only in America, but also around the world. After* Lady Liberty's *centennial restoration, her original torch was moved to her main lobby and replaced by one that is coated in twenty-four-karat gold leaf. Emma Lazarus's poem that begins, "Give me your tired, your poor," is engraved on the statue's base, which was designed by architect Richard Morris Hunt.*

Ellis Island's processing center (opposite) replaced a wooden structure destroyed by fire. The Golden Door to a new life for seventeen million Americans was abandoned to the salt air and vandals after World War II until the most ambitious restoration project in American history in the 1980s refurbished it and the Statue of Liberty. Restorers were amazed to find that of twenty-eight thousand ceiling tiles inside Ellis Island's main building (above), only seventeen required replacing. Once they were cleared to enter the United States, many immigrants proceeded to Manhattan's southernmost tip at Battery Park (overleaf). Today it's the terminus of the Staten Island Ferry as well as a hot residential neighborhood on ninety-two reclaimed acres, below Lower Manhattan's bustling financial district. Site of the first Dutch settlement of New Amsterdam, Battery Park took its name from British cannons arrayed there in the early 1600s.

The roof section of McKim, Mead & White's 1914 Beaux Arts Municipal Building alone stands ten stories high. Its huge arch straddles Chambers Street in Lower Manhattan. Once City Hall, it now houses city offices, including a marriage chapel. From there it's an easy ride— or walk—across the Brooklyn Bridge (above). The view is breathtaking from the World Trade Center observation deck (overleaf). Notable are the spires of the city's three earlier "world's tallest" sky-scrapers, the Empire State Building to the left, Chrysler Building (distant far right), and Metropolitan Life Insurance Building (foreground). In the Met Life clock, the minute hands alone are said to weigh one thousand pounds apiece.

Arturo DiModica's bronze Charging Bull *(above)*, sculpted in 1987 after a prolonged dip in stock prices, has become a symbol of optimism on New York's Wall Street. Trowbridge & Livingston added a neoclassical pediment to the New York Stock Exchange Building *(right)* in 1923. The building was elaborately designed in 1901, at the height of the nation's optimism. OPPOSITE: Inside, visitors can take a self-guided tour and peer down on the trading floor, which is less chaotic than it used to be, thanks to extensive electronic trading. The exchange was first created to handle $80 million in U.S. bonds used to pay Revolutionary War debts.

New York's most famous church, Saint Patrick's Cathedral, named for the patron saint of Ireland and home to the wealthiest Roman Catholic archdiocese in the United States, is the scene of many high-society weddings. Consecrated in 1879 but not completed until 1906, it is the shrine of the nation's first male saint, Saint John Neumann. Inside architect James Renwick Jr.'s French Gothic creation, the great baldachin, or canopy, above the high altar (opposite) is made of bronze. Its ornate, 330-foot twin spires (left) stand in marked contrast to stolid Rockefeller Center across the street, and the shiny, black-glass Olympic Tower to the rear. For decades, until the age of sky-scrapers, the spires—which were finished in 1888—dominated the midtown skyline.

Originally named the Fuller Building (right), Daniel Burnham's 1902 creation was soon renamed the Flatiron Building because of its wedge shape, only six feet wide at the apex. It overlooks Madison Square— once the city's most glamorous spot, where the city's elite "Four Hundred" dined at Delmonico's, threw parties in their nearby mansions, and attended fashionable events at Madison Square Garden. Observers felt sure that winds kicked up by its slice-shaped façade would topple the structure. The building drew crowds of males along Twenty-third Street, hoping to see ladies' ankles revealed by the swirling gusts. Police coined the phrase "Twenty-three skidoo!" to keep the oglers moving. OPPOSITE: Macy's, the world's largest department store, occupies a full city block near the Empire State Building.

Stone sentry lions guard the entrance to the New York Public Library's main building, an artistic and intellectual treasure. It was established by combining a number of private collections, including that of John Jacob Astor. The Beaux Arts structure, designed by Carrère & Hastings, cost the city $9 million when it opened in 1911. RIGHT: Henry Hardenbergh designed the landmark Plaza Hotel, overlooking Central Park off Fifth Avenue. Its rounded corner tower was the epitome of French Renaissance styling popular at the time. OPPOSITE: Jules-Alexis Coutans's sculpture of Mercury, Hercules, and Minerva was carefully refurbished during a meticulous restoration of the 1913 Grand Central Terminal in the early 1990s.

OPPOSITE: Even the Chrysler Building's gargoyles are stainless steel. William Van Alen's seventy-seven-story Art Deco jewel typified the race to be the world's tallest building. Its shining spire was hidden in the fire shaft until the unveiling, then dramatically raised to give it supremacy. More than sixteen thousand people work in the massive Art Deco Empire State Building (left), which immodestly calls itself the "Eighth Wonder of the World." ABOVE: Rockefeller Center occupies twenty-two acres of prime midtown property. The sprawling complex, whose construction began during the Great Depression, includes nineteen entertainment, shopping, and office buildings. The towering General Electric Building is its hub.

The Secretariat Building is the most recognizable landmark within the United Nations complex (above), designed by an international committee led by American Wallace Harrison. Flags of member nations ring the plaza outside, and artwork of dozens of nations abounds inside. General Assembly sessions are open to the public on a first-come, first-admitted basis. RIGHT: Park Avenue is lined with posh hotels, private palaces, and elegant apartment buildings designed by New York's top architects. Many great mansions are now international consulates, missions, and cultural institutes. Others were donated by their wealthy owners for use by charitable and other not-for-profit agencies.

Catching a play in the theater district is a handy excuse for a visit to Manhattan. Television shows are produced there as well; top entertainment personalities can be spotted in and around the Ed Sullivan Theater (above) on Broadway. RIGHT: Times Square—long known as the "Crossroads of the World"—degenerated for a time into a peep-show row and hangout for prostitutes. But the square, which is actually triangular, has been substantially sanitized, and big corporations are underwriting new ventures throughout the neon district. Radio City Music Hall (opposite), is part of the Rockefeller Center complex. There, at Christmas and Easter, the high-stepping Rockettes still perform. OVERLEAF: The glittering Tavern on the Green is a rare commercial enterprise in Central Park.

Architect Calvert Vaux and landscape architect Frederick Law Olmsted collaborated on the design of New York's "backyard"—Central Park, which replaced miserable bogs and squatters' shacks and is, by law, forever protected from development. Figures from Hans Christian Andersen to Alice in Wonderland are remembered with statues in the park. Yoko Ono paid to have a section restored as the international Strawberry Fields peace garden in memory of her slain husband, John Lennon. Paul Manship's 1932 bronze Group of Bears (above) stands just inside Central Park. OVERLEAF: The statue in the reflecting pool of the park's Conservatory Garden is of Mary and Dickon from Frances Hodgson Burnett's classic The Secret Garden. Thousands of tulips bloom in the garden each spring, and thousands more chrysanthemums appear each fall.

Columbus Avenue (opposite) on the Upper West Side was once a grungy tenement district. It has come alive with eclectic flea markets, sidewalk cafés, and glitzy boutiques featuring what Fodor's guide calls "high funk." ABOVE: John Lennon lived at the Dakota on Central Park West and was murdered by a deranged fan outside its entrance in 1980. The first Upper West Side luxury apartment building was erected in the 1880s by Edward Clark, heir to the Singer sewing machine fortune. Locals called it "Clark's Folly" because of its location, out in the "country," far from city grandeur. Friends said he might as well have chosen far-away Dakota Territory, and the name stuck. But the grandeur quickly moved north to this part of town. The building's thick walls, massive floors, and heavy interior partitions make it one of New York's quietest residences.

Several famous architects, including Calvert Vaux and John Russell Pope, had a hand in the design and expansions of the American Museum of Natural History (left). Its more than thirty-six million artifacts include meteor fragments, lifelike dioramas, and a huge dinosaur collection. ABOVE: The memorial to Union general Ulysses Grant, popularly known as "Grant's Tomb," also holds the remains of the general's wife.

John Duncan's white-granite mausoleum is modeled after Napoleon's final resting place, Les Invalides in Paris. Bronze busts in the crypt depict Grant's subordinates. Inside the Cloisters (overleaf), the Metropolitan Museum of Art's medieval-style annex in Fort Tryon Park, a fifteenth-century Spanish tempera and oil triptych hangs above a German altarpiece, c. 1470, and busts of female saints.

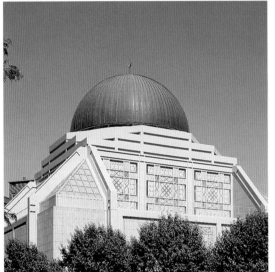

The Reform Jewish Congregation Emanu-El settled into the largest synagogue in the United States (left)—and one of the largest in the world—seating 2,500 worshipers (more than Saint Patrick's Cathedral) on East Sixty-fifth at Fifth Avenue. The building, designed by Kohn, Butler, and Stein in 1929, shows Romanesque, Byzantine, Moorish, and even Art Deco influences. It occupies a site where a grand mansion belonging to Caroline Astor once stood. ABOVE: The architects Skidmore, Owings & Merrill used a computer to be certain the 1991 gray-granite Islamic Center of New York—the city's first large-scale mosque—faces Mecca, as required by Islamic law. It serves the city's 400,000 Muslims as well as diplomats and visitors from Muslim nations.

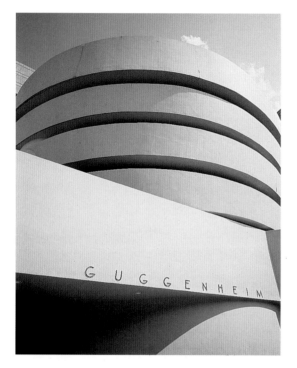

Tours of Frank Lloyd Wright's 1959 Guggenheim Museum (above) begin at the top and proceed down a spiraling hallway. The building houses Solomon R. Guggenheim's collection originally gathered at the "Museum of Non-Objective Paintings," as well as ample sculptures. Roman emperor Augustus built the Temple of Dendur (right), now on display at the Metropolitan Museum of Art, which spans almost 1.5 million square feet and includes more than three million works of art. OVERLEAF: Scottish immigrant Archibald Gracie, who made a fortune in the shipping business, built a home on the East River in 1799. It became a city museum, and then, beginning with Fiorello La Guardia, the mayor's residence.

Upper East Side brownstones (opposite) are among the city's most fashionable. (Remember the theme song to The Jeffersons *television show? "Movin' on up, to the East Side.") The* area, especially along Fifth Avenue, once home to breweries and factories, became "Millionaires' Row" as the wealthy fled ethnic encroachment downtown. Bistros such as Trois Jean *(above) on East Seventy-ninth Street captured New Yorkers' taste for simple, yet exotic, food, often fused from several cultures.* OVERLEAF: *Galleries, clothing and curio shops, grocery* stores, and restaurants abound in Chinatown, which has expanded from three to more than forty square blocks. Its more than 150,000 residents make New York's Chinatown not only larger than *San Francisco's, but also the largest Chinese community outside of Asia. Tortuously narrow and crooked streets are especially crowded around Chinese New Year in mid-winter.*

The size of Little Italy (opposite) has shrunk as Chinatown expands. Savory holdouts, including restaurants, cheese shops, and delicatessens, can be found along Mulberry Street. In Greenwich Village, even the firehouses (top left) are charming. Cheap rents attracted writers like Walt Whitman and artists like John La Farge. The Access NYC guide calls the Village "the birthplace of the bohemian spirit." BOTTOM: M. Chemiakin's 1993 bronze Cybele: Goddess of Fertility is a prominent fixture at Mimi Ferzt's gallery in artsy SoHo. Greene Street (overleaf) is a warren of antique shops, studios, and loft apartments. Just over a quarter of a century ago, the area was a virtual wasteland of grimy, often abandoned, warehouses. Preservationists saved the world's largest concentration of cast-iron architecture.

Sylvia's Restaurant (opposite), named for Sylvia Woods, the "Queen of Soul Food," is patronized as much by tourists as by locals. The new Cotton Club nightclub (left) replaced a Harlem entertainment institution where downtown whites pulled up in limousines to hear Duke Ellington, Cab Calloway, and other legendary musicians. The club's replacement still features blues and jazz on "Harlem's Main Street" under the entryway to the George Washington Bridge. Convent Avenue (Page 74) in Hamilton Heights is lined with neat townhouses. The nation's first U.S. secretary of the treasury, Alexander Hamilton, built a home there, and Hamilton Heights was developed after the elevated railroad made its way to far-north Manhattan. Sylvan Terrace (Page 75), off Roger Morris Park, is one of Harlem's finest addresses.

Yankee Stadium in the Bronx (preceding pages) is the "House that [Babe] Ruth Built"—and owner George Steinbrenner renovated. The fortunes of the team once called the "Bronx Bombers" seemed to mirror those of the borough: like the Bronx, the Yanks went downhill in the 1980s, only to rebound in the last decade of the century. Just up the hill from Yankee Stadium, a relief sets a heroic tone at the Bronx Courthouse (top right). The Hall of Fame for Great Americans (bottom) at Bronx Community College stands on the highest natural point in New York City. It was dedicated in 1901 as a pantheon honoring historically significant men and women. Pictured is the Scientist and Inventor Wing. OPPOSITE: The upper Bronx holds innumerable surprises, including elegant homes.

Theodore Roosevelt, Arturo Toscanini, and Mark Twain were all brief tenants of Wave Hill, the former estate of financier and conservationist George Perkins in the upper Bronx along the Hudson. The estate, which was given to the city in 1965 and is often used for concerts, features a restful garden (opposite), designed by Viennese landscape gardener Albert Millard. ABOVE: Founded in 1891, the 250-acre New York Botanical Garden in the Bronx completely refurbished its 1902 Enid A. Haupt Conservatory in the late 1990s. The conservatory, modeled after London's Crystal Palace, is a center of environmental research as well as a showcase of plants from around the world. In the foreground is a section of the Jane Watson Irwin Perennial Garden, arranged in patterns according to shade, color, height, and blooming season. The botanical garden's café is a converted 1840 snuff mill.

The "Rainey Gates" (left) open into the Bronx Zoo (now properly called the International Wildlife Conservation Park), America's largest urban zoo. The gates, erected in 1933 by sculptor Paul Manship in the French Arts Decoratifs *style*, was dedicated in memory of big-game hunter and zoo patron Paul J. Rainey. ABOVE: Monkeys, tapirs, leopards, and other species live in JungleWorld, a re-created Southeast Asian rain forest, mangrove swamp, and scrub forest. In recent years the zoo, which was founded in 1899, has concentrated on housing vanishing species and perpetuating endangered creatures such as the snow leopard. It operates satellite wildlife centers in Queens, Manhattan's Central Park, and Brooklyn's Prospect Park.

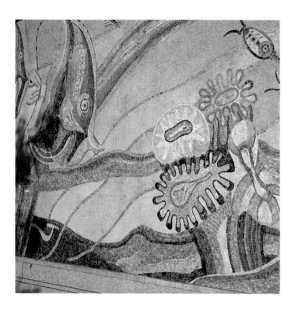

The mosaic above appears on a building along the Bronx's Grand Concourse, designed in 1892 to connect Manhattan with its new "annexed district." Dozens of Art Deco and Art Moderne apartment buildings appeared along the four-mile-long raised "speedway" in the 1930s. Several winning entries in the America's Cup sailing races were built in boathouses on City Island (right), the Bronx's taste of New England on Long Island Sound. The island is wildly eclectic: next door to the weathered North Wind Undersea Institute Museum is an old sea captain's home that has been turned into Le Refuge Bed & Breakfast, run by Pierre Saint-Denis, one of Manhattan's renowned chefs. OVERLEAF: Queens is one of the few remaining places where the "subway" (overleaf) is still elevated in spots.

Steinway pianos (opposite) are still made only in Queens and in Hamburg, Germany, just as they were when German immigrant Wilhelm Steinweg moved his manufacturing plant from Park Avenue in Manhattan to a spot on the East River. The Waldorf-Astoria Hotel was built on the Manhattan site, and Steinweg created a virtual company town in Queens. Master craftsman William Steinway (his Americanized name) became a fast friend of Grover Cleveland and gave the president a grand piano as a wedding gift. Steinway's mansion, built in Astoria, still stands. Shea Stadium (above) was built on a dumpsite called Flushing Meadows. The stadium hosted a Beatles concert in 1965, two years after it opened, and a mass by Pope John Paul II in 1979. After the amazing Mets baseball team of 1986 won a pennant and then a World Series, the stadium was painted a piercing Met blue.

The New York Hall of Science and the Unisphere (opposite), relics of the 1964 World's Fair, can be found in Flushing Meadows Corona Park in Queens. The Hall of Science was the fair's Science Pavilion. Its interactive displays and video screens that can magnify microscopic particles delight visitors. The undulating building, clad in concrete panels studded with stained glass, is itself a curiosity. The 380-ton Unisphere, designed by Peter Muller-Munk, Inc., features a grid representing the earth as well as orbiting satellites. Wading in its reflecting pool is almost de rigeuer for children visiting Corona Park. OVERLEAF: Nearly hidden off Vernon Boulevard along the East River in Queens is the Socrates Sculpture Park, a seemingly haphazard collection of sculptures that frame the Manhattan skyline most unusually. Fodor's guide says its abstract artwork "first appears almost as an urban hallucination."

Jackson Heights in Queens (opposite) was the ultimate "urban suburbia." Begun in the 1920s as America's first large-scale garden apartment community, the neighborhood of block after block of apartment complexes has retained its architectural integrity. Financed by Edward MacDougall and designed by architects Andrew J. Thomas and George Wells, Jackson Heights rose on three hundred acres of farmland. The idea was to make densely packed urban spaces livable. The developers considered each block a "planning unit," to include playgrounds and houses of worship as well as residences. Apartments were owned rather than rented and only to carefully screened buyers of means. LEFT: Landscaped courtyard gardens, such as those at The Towers, were owned in common. MacDougall liked The Towers so much that he moved in.

The boroughs outside Manhattan are full of ethnic surprises. Greek restaurants, grocery stores, and shops like this nail salon (opposite) abound in the Astoria section of Queens. Authentic Italian markets (top left) tempt the taste buds along Arthur Avenue in the Belmont-Arthur section of the Bronx. Parts of Main Street in Flushing, Queens, have become virtual Asian bazaars (bottom), where vendors serve delicacies like Chinese steamed dumplings. OVERLEAF: Hidden among Brooklyn's tall buildings, as seen from South Street Seaport in Manhattan, are many ethnic culinary and fashion delights, an easy subway ride away. Brooklyn's Cobble Hill neighborhood, for instance, is crammed with Italian restaurants and shops, which fill Court Street with the intoxicating smells of pasta, cheeses, olives, and sauces.

Grand Army Plaza (page 100) in Brooklyn's Park Slope is anchored by the Soldiers' and Sailors' Memorial Arch, inspired by the Arc de Triomphe in Paris. Frederick McMonnies created the heroic four-horse chariot. Richard Upjohn designed the ornate Gothic gateway to Brooklyn's Green-Wood Cemetery (page 101), where many New York notables— Samuel F. B. Morse,

Nathaniel Currier, and James Ives, among them— found eternal rest. The New York Transit Museum (above), in an abandoned Brooklyn station, offers plenty of chances to catch an informative "ride." McKim, Mead & White designed the Brooklyn Museum building (right) in 1897. The museum's African and pre-Columbian collections are world-renowned.

America's oldest performing-arts center is the Brooklyn Academy of Music (above, with detail opposite). Its 1908 Renaissance Revival building includes an opera house, symphony hall— a showcase for the Brooklyn Symphony Orchestra—and chamber-music hall. The building's stolid appearance belies the academy's willingness to experiment with avant-garde performances. Each autumn, it produces a festival of provocative works called "New Wave." The organization also stages numerous children's musical and stage performances. Little wonder Brooklynites feel free to call their music and dance center simply, "BAM." In 1987, the academy reopened and refurbished the then-eighty-three-year-old Majestic Theater, which was a decaying movie house before it closed in 1967. The AIA Guide to New York City *described the Academy complex— which has become a recognized historic district—as "a veritable Vesuvius of talent in dance, theater, and music."*

Halsey, McCormack & Helmer's 1929 Williamsburgh Savings Bank Tower (right) dominates the Brooklyn landscape. Replete with Romanesque columns, arches, and capitals, the building is still a popular office complex. It includes a twenty-sixth-floor outdoor observation patio. Williamsburgh was an independent town annexed by Brooklyn in the 1850s—forty years before Brooklyn itself was absorbed into Greater New York. OPPOSITE: Thomas H. Jones designed the screen over the entryway to the 1941 Brooklyn Public Library's main branch on Grand Army Plaza at Flatbush Avenue and Eastern Parkway on the edge of Prospect Park. The neighborhood was reserved by planners Frederick Law Olmsted and Calvert Vaux for a series of institutions, including the library, the Brooklyn Museum, and the Brooklyn Botanic Garden.

Warren Place is one of many verdant nooks on Brooklyn's Cobble Hill (left), where the Continental Army once dug in for the Battle of Brooklyn. When Brooklyn Heights became too expensive for many young professionals, they found affordable housing a little farther from the Brooklyn Bridge in Cobble Hill. Warren Place's "cottages for the workingman" were built in 1878 and 1879 under the sponsorship of Alfred Tredway White, a Brooklyn businessman and philanthropist interested in replacing tenement houses with decent, affordable units.

ABOVE: Block after block of classic brownstones are more in vogue than ever in Park Slope, named for its setting on the downward slant from Prospect Park.

The Dyker Heights neighborhood of Brooklyn is full of character—including distinctively landscaped homes, both large and small. The unit on Eighty-sixth Street (opposite) was one of many built by Donald Trump's father, Fred. Several houses along Eleventh Avenue (above) and elsewhere in Dyker Heights have the look of the Black Forest about them.

The Heights overlook the Verrazano Narrows and Gravesend Bay, with a good view of Staten Island. OVERLEAF: Borough—sometimes spelled Boro— Park includes a large Jewish enclave, including thousands of second-generation Hasidic Jews who patronize shops along Thirteenth Avenue. The area had been parkland, set among several of Brooklyn's villages within the old Dutch town of New Utrecht. Borough Park was developed in the 1920s and grew rapidly because of its ready access to the West End subway line.

Brooklyn's Coney Island (left), the "World's Largest Playground," first drew fun-seekers from throughout the boroughs because of its unbeatable one-two punch: a rollicking amusement park and fine Atlantic Ocean beaches. Some say Coney Island hot dogs alone are still worth a visit. The subway's arrival in 1920, soon followed by completion of the park's boardwalk, sealed its popularity, which withstood the Depression, deterioration of the old wooden roller coasters, and construction of public housing just across the road. Next door is New York's Aquarium (above), a branch of the Wildlife Conservation Society. Its Conservation Hall features colorful exhibits from the Belize Coral Reefs, the Amazon River, and the depths of several oceans.

Brighton Beach is a largely Russian section of Brooklyn on the eastern edge of what had been a larger Coney Island. A giant resort hotel, since demolished, once occupied the beachfront. Part of the beach itself (above) lies at the foot of "Neil Sedaka Way," named for the pop singer whose parents owned a hot dog stand at the foot of Coney Island Avenue. (Each year at a festival, nostalgic Brooklyn makes a point of saluting ex-Brooklynites who have earned fame in show business and elsewhere.) Brighton Beach Avenue (opposite) is known as "Little Odessa." Almost one hundred thousand Russian, Ukrainian, and Georgian Jews and other emigrés live in the area and crowd into its delis and affordable borscht and blini joints. Kingsborough Community College has taken over the old Naval Training Station at the tip of Brighton Beach.

Staten Islanders were happy with their ferry (left), though not always with the frequency of service. There was little groundswell for a bridge to other boroughs, but one was built anyway. The Verrazano-Narrows Bridge brought tens of thousands of new residents, mostly from Brooklyn, to which it connected, and also development that quickened the pace of life on the previously drowsy island. One link to the past, however, is Historic Richmond Town— twenty-seven authentic and historic buildings, including the remarkably restored 1837 Stephens's General Store (overleaf). Richmond Town was the bustling seat of the original county of that name that comprised Staten Island. Special programs on the area's history, agriculture, commerce, and maritime life are offered year-round there.

Staten Island is a largely unassuming place. Eateries like the Cargo Café (left) on Bay Street in Saint George offer simple but delectable home-style fare. Even the Richmond Terrace Produce Stand attracts customers to its bountiful local fruits and vegetables with catchy homemade signs (above). Truck farms used to be numerous before developers gobbled up acres of available land for houses, shopping malls, and commercial strips. Though life on the island has turned somewhat prosaic, it was historically a lively and intriguing place. During the American Revolution, for instance, the island was the base of operations for thirty thousand British troops who defeated General George Washington's colonial army on both Manhattan and Long Island.

Some of Staten Island's large Roman Catholic population has been served since 1919 by Saint Peter's Church, a detail of which is shown above. Somehow, the sanctuary, rectory, and bell tower all manage to hug a steep cliff overlooking Richmond Terrace in Saint George. Carefully restored houses like this one in Tottenville (right) can be found throughout Staten Island. The home was built in 1892 by John Brown's shipyard workers as a wedding gift to Brown and his bride. OVERLEAF: In the Livingston neighborhood, the old Sailors Snug Harbor— a maritime hospital and home for retired sailors—has been converted into serene Snug Harbor, which includes acres of parkland, fountains, and performance halls.

Index

One of New York's most amazing museum exhibits is the Panorama of the City of New York, a permanent attraction at the Queens Museum of Art.

This 9,335-square-foot model of all 320 square miles of New York City includes more than 850,000 tiny houses, office towers, bridges, and other structures.